Get out of bed! It's time for...

THE AWFUL AIR TRAVEL ACTIVITY BOOK

By Andy Robbins

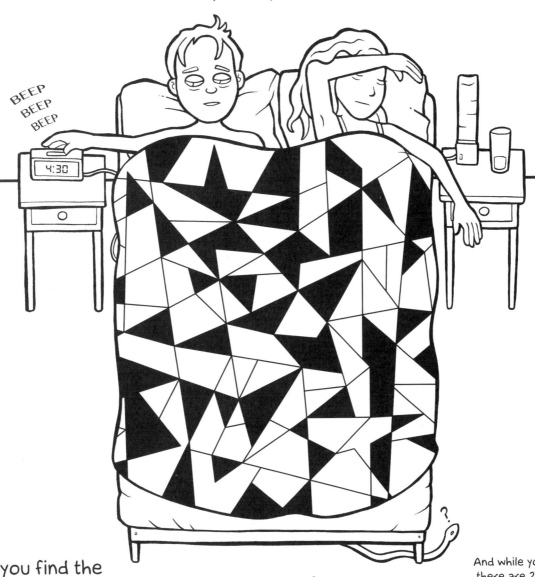

BEEP
BEEP
BEEP

Can you find the
star hidden in
the quilt?

FARCOUNTRY
PRESS

And while you're at it,
there are 20 snakes
(including this one)
slithering around the
book. Can you locate all
of them?

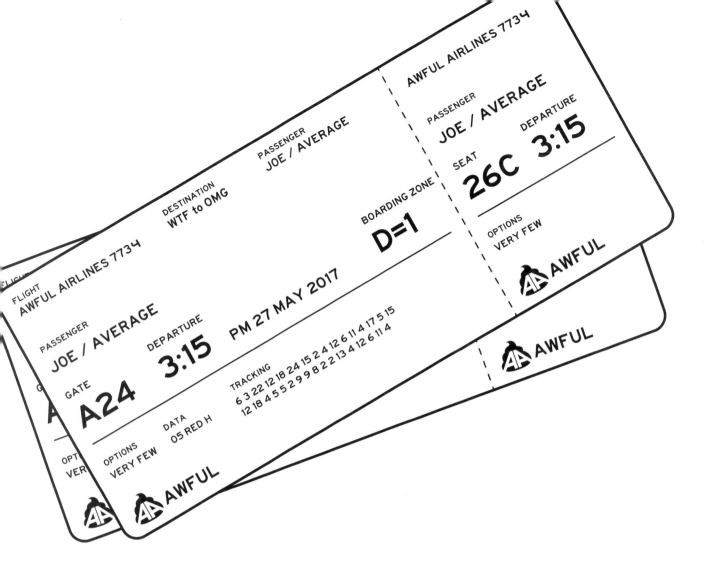

ISBN: 978-1-56037-708-5

© 2017 by Farcountry Press
Text and Illustrations © 2017 Andy Robbins, www.andyrobbinsart.com

For more information about our books, contact Farcountry Press, P.O. Box 5630, Helena, MT 59604 or call (800) 821-3874; or visit www.farcountrypress.com.

 Produced and printed in the United States of America.

21   20   19   18   17   1   2   3   4   5

It's time to leave for the airport, but it looks like you might be forgetting something!
Use the items in the picture as clues to find the 23 words hidden below!

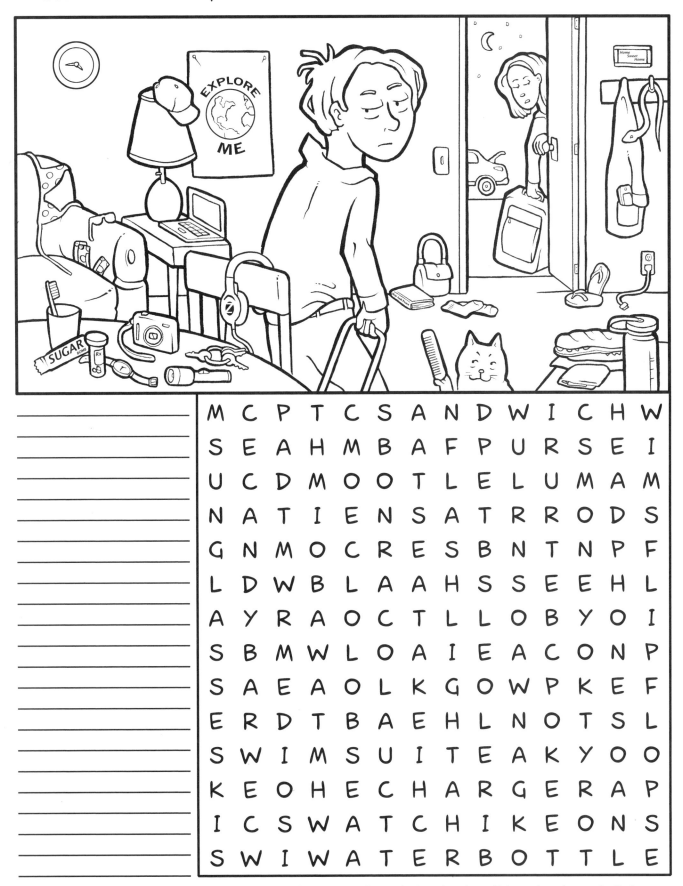

M	C	P	T	C	S	A	N	D	W	I	C	H	W
S	E	A	H	M	B	A	F	P	U	R	S	E	I
U	C	D	M	O	O	T	L	E	L	U	M	A	M
N	A	T	I	E	N	S	A	T	R	R	O	D	S
G	N	M	O	C	R	E	S	B	N	T	N	P	F
L	D	W	B	L	A	A	H	S	S	E	E	H	L
A	Y	R	A	O	C	T	L	L	O	B	Y	O	I
S	B	M	W	L	O	A	I	E	A	C	O	N	P
S	A	E	A	O	L	K	G	O	W	P	K	E	F
E	R	D	T	B	A	E	H	L	N	O	T	S	L
S	W	I	M	S	U	I	T	E	A	K	Y	O	O
K	E	O	H	E	C	H	A	R	G	E	R	A	P
I	C	S	W	A	T	C	H	I	K	E	O	N	S
S	W	I	W	A	T	E	R	B	O	T	T	L	E

I see my mother in my face, but only when I travel. - Amanda Palmer

You need to park your car... but where? All the lots are full except the one farthest from the airport, and it's filling up quickly! Fill all of the empty parking spaces with vehicles (or their respective numbers) so that only one of each type of vehicle appears in each row, column, and box of six. After successfully parking, you'll have an agonizing fifteen-minute wait for the crowded shuttle bus to finally deliver you to the check-in counter.

SECURITY NIGHTMARE!

CANCER SCAN

TIPS

Help TSA find all of the contraband hidden in the above scene!

arrow
hammer
box cutter
bigger knife
pistol
dynamite

katana
mace
shotgun
straight razor
pointy knife

rubber chicken
revolver
knife
saw

dynamite
axe
derringer
gun
bomb
brass knuckles
axe
taser

cleaver
time bomb
nunchucks
throwing star
oversized yogurt
pepper spray
grenade
bat
scissors

CHOOSE YOUR COLOR BY NUMBER

The "If you can't trust a senior citizen, who can you trust?" COLOR SCHEME	
1. Yellow	6. Red
2. Yellow	7. Lavender
3. Yellow	8. Lavender
4. Red	9. Lavender
5. Red	

The "I know a terrorist when I see one!" COLOR SCHEME	
1. Red	6. Red
2. Grey	7. Red
3. Light Blue	8. Light Blue
4. Light Blue	9. Grey
5. Grey	

Travel is only glamorous in retrospect. - Paul Theroux

AIRPORT SCAVENGER HUNT

Got a little time before your flight or an extra long layover? Take a walk around the concourse and see how many of these items you can find! If you have a friend who'd like to play too, have him or her photograph this page with a phone and use it to see who can collect the most points!

A sleeping person, +3 points. -3 points if you wake him up.

POINTS

A "therapy" dog, +3 points. +2 bonus if it's an actual service animal.

POINTS

An unapologetically loud phone talker, +1 point each.

POINTS

A clean bathroom stall, +3 points.

POINTS

Someone getting a ride in a wheelchair, +2 points.

POINTS

A piece of fruit, +2 points.

A neck pillow, +2 points.

POINTS

A cart in a hurry, +3 points. +1 point for a stationary one.

POINTS

A sports team, + ½ point per member.

POINTS

A courtesy telephone, +1 point. +2 bonus if it's white.

COURTESY PHONE

POINTS

A food service employee you can't understand, +3 points.

POINTS

A potted plant +2 points. +2 bonus if it's real.

POINTS

A moving sidewalk, +2 points. +3 bonus if you walk the length of one backwards.

POINTS

YOU CAN DO IT!

A running person, +3 points. +2 bonus if you offer encouragement.

POINTS

+1 point for every flight on the departures board that is delayed.

POINTS

DEPARTURES
CANCUN.............DELAYED
ORLANDO...........DELAYED
SAN DIEGO.........DELAYED
MAUI..................DELAYED
DETROIT.............ON TIME

A child on a leash, +4 points.

POINTS

A flight crew on their way to a gate, +3 points.

POINTS

TOTAL SCORE

How'd you do? Tally up your points to determine your final score!

START

END

Nothing says traveling like eating a greasy lunch before getting on a bumpy airplane. You want two slices of pizza and you want them to be EXACTLY alike. Can you find the perfect pair?

Concourse Maze: You need to get to your gate, but want to make a few stops along the way. Visit the bathroom, pick up some pizza, grab a bottle of water, and buy a book IN THAT ORDER before heading to your gate. Line must pass through an object to collect it, lines may not cross or touch, and no backtracking. Can you do it?

Fun Fact: A commercial jet reaches speeds of up to 180 mph during take-off!

Word Flow

Use the names of all 11 US-based airlines (as of 2017) to fill in the blanks. Transfer letters from one word to another via the connecting lines. Finally, use the letters in the numbered boxes to find the answer to the joke below!

Fun Fact: A 747 is made up of 6 million parts!

Row 1: _ _ _ [1] K _ _
Row 2: _ _ _ B[2] _ _ _
Row 3: _ _ [3] _ _ W _ _ _
Row 4: [9] P _ [5] _ _ _
Row 5: _ _ _ T _ _ _
Row 6: _ _ [4] _ _ _
Row 7: _ _ _ _ G[7] _ _ _ _
Row 8: _ _ _ _ _ _ _ _ [6]
Row 9: _ _ _ _ _ C[8] _ _
Row 10: _ _ O _ _ [10] _ _ _
Row 11: _ _ _ _ _ [11]

What do you get when you cross a snake with a plane?

□ □□□□□□
1   2 3 4 5 6 7

□□□□□□□□□□□□
8 3 6 9 10 11 5 8 10 3 11

11

EVERYONE AT THE AIRPORT IS USING A CELLPHONE!

Everyone, that is, except for four people; can you find them? Can you also spot a confused president, a canine caller, three self-absorbed selfies, two robots, a superhero stand-off, a two-way call, and an expectant phone user?

Long Wait at the Gate!

Recommended Colors:
No Go Indigo
Terminal Gray
Beige Without End
The Color of Despair

13

Uh-Oh! The flight at this gate has been delayed, maybe even cancelled. Just look at all those unhappy faces! The two pictures below contain 21 differences. Can you spot them all?

PRE-FLIGHT CROSSWORD

14 Down: The nearest one may be behind you

8 Across: Though oxygen is flowing, the mask may not _____

7 Down: Default seat belt status

1 Across: Type of aircraft features I'm about to demonstrate

Across
4. Flight attendants, ready for departure
6. Tray table landing position
10. No tampering with, disabling, or destroying
12. The chances of a water landing
13. Built of aluminum, not logs
15. Use when opening overhead bins

Down
2. Sit back, relax, and attempt to enjoy this
3. Do this with carry-ons
5. Portable, electronic
9. Prepare doors for _____
11. Fasten Seat Belt sign master

Note: Flight attendant enthusiasm may vary.

Q: What do you call it when you're sick of being in the airport? A: Terminal Sickness!

Fun Fact: Food tastes different on an airplane because the change in air pressure numbs about a third of your taste buds!

Watch-Out Tower

Probably Dinner

START

Air Mail

B29

People Injector

Captain's Sleeping Quarters

Flight Attendant Gossip Lounge

Rubber Ground Banger

Re-accommodated Passenger

Overstuffed Boxes of Your Junk

Toothy Terrorist

AWFUL AIRLINES

CONNECT THE DOTS!

Begin with dot #1 and connect the dots in numeric order to complete the picture. When you reach an open circle, take your pencil off the paper and stop. Look around the page to locate the next consecutive number and continue connecting the dots from that point!

When you're done, see if you can find a person or an object that begins with every letter of the alphabet, from A to Z!

Unauthorized Arrival

AWFUl

Primary Germ Dispersal Chamber

Ew.

Butt

Jet-Powered
Bird Blender

Gravity Defying
Magic Triangles

Very Important
Passenger

BRAINSSSS:

AWFUL AIRLINES

Fire Juice Truck

END

Suspicious
Baggage

It can hardly be a coincidence that no language on Earth has ever produced the expression "As pretty as an airport."
- Douglas Adams

INFLIGHT SCAVENGER HUNT

While not as varied as a search inside the terminal, a hunt onboard the airplane can still be fun. Complete activities and locate special passengers during your flight for a big score!

The bulk of mankind is as well equipped for flying as thinking.
- Jonathan Swift

How'd you do? Tally up your points to determine your final score!

Inflight Plight!

Recommended Colors:
Orange We There Yet?
Not Well Yellow
Red-Eye Blue
Boxed-In Brown

The captain has turned off the Fasten Seat Belt sign! It is now safe to block the aisle, visit the lavatory repeatedly, and rummage through the overhead bins! The two pictures below contain 21 differences. Can you spot them all?

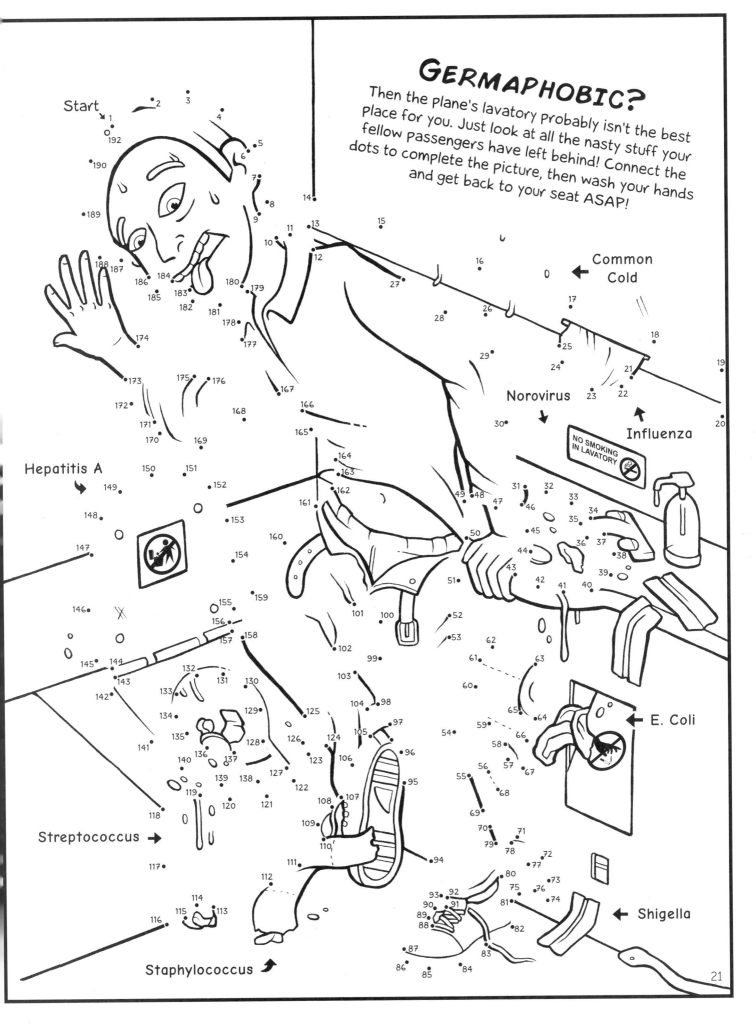

GERMAPHOBIC?

Then the plane's lavatory probably isn't the best place for you. Just look at all the nasty stuff your fellow passengers have left behind! Connect the dots to complete the picture, then wash your hands and get back to your seat ASAP!

Start

Common Cold

Norovirus

Influenza

Hepatitis A

E. Coli

NO SMOKING IN LAVATORY

Streptococcus

Shigella

Staphylococcus

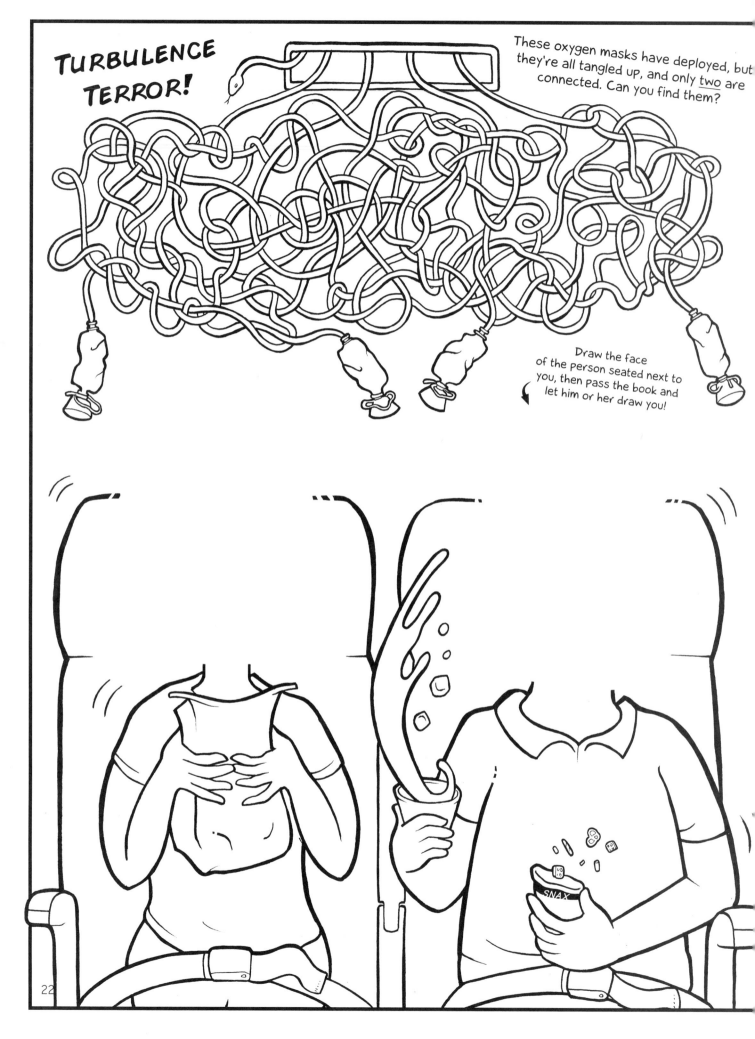

WHAT KIND OF PASSENGER ARE YOU?
Take our handy quiz and find out!

1. Your flight has arrived at the gate, and the door has finally been opened. But the line isn't moving! **You:**

   A) Complain loudly while doing a jig of impatience.

   B) Let out a primal howl and plow through the people in front of you. Comin' through!

   C) Wait your turn while smiling wearily at those around you.

   D) Have a seat until everyone else disembarks. You're just going to have to stand around at baggage claim anyway.

2. Your flight gets stuck on the tarmac for several hours with no updates from the flight crew. **You:**

   A) Sigh. A lot.

   B) Crack open the latest espionage novel and get some reading done.

   C) Unsuccessfully visualize your happy place. Succumb to despair.

   D) Attempt to take the flight deck by force, get tased, and end up on the evening news.

3. The passenger seated beside you has brought her "therapy" pig onboard. **You:**

   A) Lick your lips and murmur "Baconnnnn" until the pig owner asks to be reseated.

   B) Toss the pig out the door before it closes. No pigs on *your* plane!

   C) Ignore the pig until its self-esteem is crushed.

   D) Get to know the pig. It's going to be a long flight, and you are seatmates, after all.

4. You've more or less successfully used the lavatory, but there's no soap OR water to wash up. **You:**

   A) Resolve not to touch your face for the rest of the trip. Or any food. Or your phone. Or maybe anything.

   B) Return to your seat and bathe in the hand sanitizer you've brought with you.

   C) Lick your fingers clean. It's all over at this point anyway. The germs have won.

   D) Shrug. Who washes their hands anyway?

5. The baby behind you is a snotty, noisy brat who won't stop crying. **You:**

   A) Threaten to throw the annoying youngster through a window if he doesn't shut up.

   B) Relax. It's not *your* kid crying, so whatev.

   C) Do a little crying yourself.

   D) Use your baby whisperer magic to soothe the child.

6. Your flight's started its descent, but *OMG*, you're 63% sure you need to use the bathroom! **You:**

   A) Hold it. You'll be on the ground in 20 minutes and you can go then.

   B) Battle your way to the lavatory, stiff-arming aside other weak-bladdered passengers.

   C) Pee into your empty water bottle like a trucker.

   D) Calmly make your way to the lavatory, willing the Fasten Seat Belt sign to stay off.

7. Your flight encounters a nasty stretch of turbulence. **You:**

   A) Frantically remove all of your clothing so you can swim better if the plane crashes into water.

   B) Vomit all over your seatmate, *Exorcist*-style.

   C) Wonder how up to date your Last Will and Testament really is.

   D) Sit back and focus your chi. You'll survive.

8. You stumble upon some unattended baggage in the terminal. **You:**

   A) Barely have time to get a gyro, let alone report unattended baggage.

   B) Tackle the unattended baggage before it can hurt anyone.

   C) Console the luggage. Maybe it's lost.

   D) Report the unattended baggage in gaspy tones to the nearest airport employee.

Add up your points!

1. A) 3 B) 4 C) 2 D) 1
2. A) 2 B) 1 C) 3 D) 4
3. A) 3 B) 4 C) 2 D) 1
4. A) 2 B) 1 C) 4 D) 3
5. A) 4 B) 2 C) 3 D) 1
6. A) 1 B) 3 C) 4 D) 2
7. A) 4 B) 3 C) 2 D) 1
8. A) 1 B) 4 C) 3 D) 2

8-12 points:
Ultimate Flyer
You are exceptionally well prepared for the tribulations of modern air travel.

13-20 points:
Typical Airline Patron
You're going to get from point A to point B in one piece and that's all you're really worried about.

21-28 points:
Awful Air Traveler
You're one flight cancellation away from a YouTube-worthy meltdown.

29+ points:
Unstable Passenger
You are a liability to yourself and others. Consider driving next time.

A **REBUS PUZZLE** is a picture made with letters and words that represents a common phrase. Can you figure these out?

SECURITY

LUGGAGE
carry

FLIGHT FLIGHT

GATE

LANDING

INITIAL

couchecknter

FLIGHT
SOLD

class ←
class
class

curb check-in

TRAVELING
c c c c c c

FLIGHT
MAGAZINE

ARRIVAL
TIME

BIN
HEAD

What Goes Up Must Come Down! Use the color scheme of your choice to finish the picture. Color the jet however you like!

Worst-Case Scenario
Coloring Scheme

1 - Black   6 - Dark Blue
2 - Black   7 - Light Blue
3 - Black   8 - Yellow
4 - White   9 - Red/Orange
5 - Dark Blue   10 - Gray

Ack, No Way! Happy Ending
Coloring Scheme

1 - Pink   6 - Dark Gray
2 - Yellow   7 - Green
3 - Sky Blue   8 - Sky Blue
4 - Sky Blue   9 - Sky Blue
5 - Brown   10 - Sky Blue

There is nothing safer than flying. It's crashing that is dangerous. - Theo Cowan

LET ME OUTTA HERE!

The best part about getting on a plane is getting off at the end of the flight. Sometimes it takes awhile for the line to move, though. The picture below contains 35 silly or just plain wrong things to help you lighten up. Can you find them all?

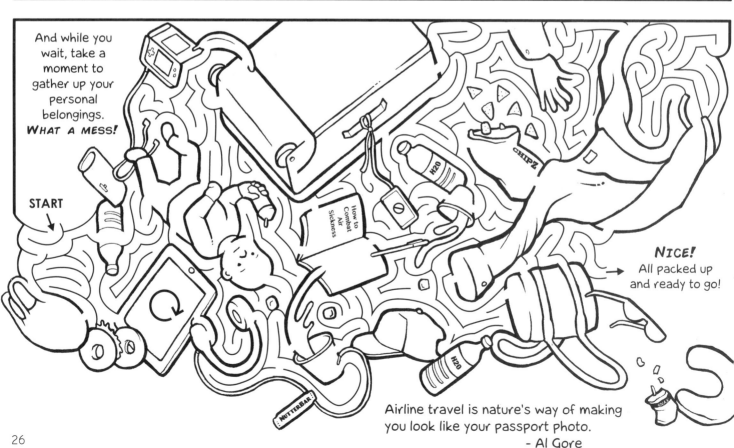

And while you wait, take a moment to gather up your personal belongings. **WHAT A MESS!**

START

NICE!
All packed up and ready to go!

Airline travel is nature's way of making you look like your passport photo.
- Al Gore

Two of these six carry-ons are identical. Can you find them?

HERE COMES THE BAGGAGE!

Everyone's waiting for his or her baggage. Match each passenger with the items they've shipped beneath the plane!

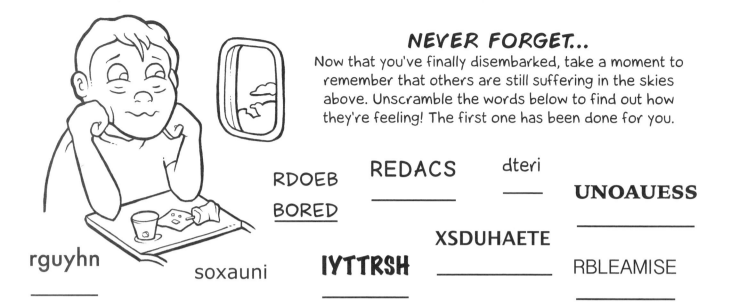

NEVER FORGET...

Now that you've finally disembarked, take a moment to remember that others are still suffering in the skies above. Unscramble the words below to find out how they're feeling! The first one has been done for you.

RDOEB
BORED

REDACS
_____

dteri
____

UNOAUESS
_____

rguyhn
_____

soxauni
_____

IYTTRSH
_____

XSDUHAETE
_____

RBLEAMISE
_____

AIRLINE MISPLACE YOUR LUGGAGE AGAIN?

Use the provided patterns (or make your own) to customize and color a new set of luggage. Don't forget to add your monogram to the nameplates!

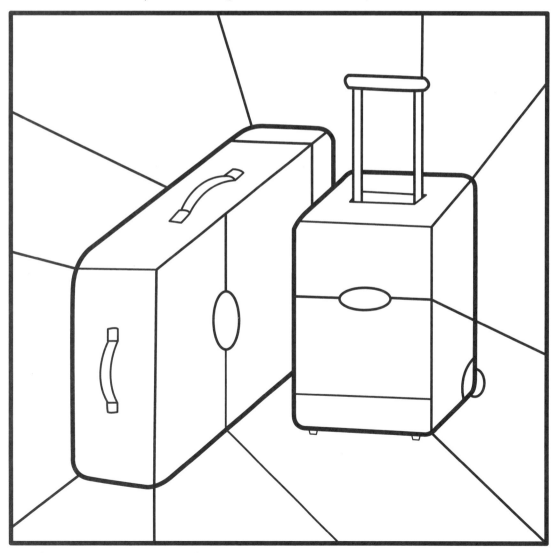

Why buy good luggage? You only use it when you travel. - Yogi Berra

AWFUL AIRLINES

SEAL OF SUBPAR PERFORMANCE · SEAL OF SUBPAR PERFORMANCE · SEAL OF SUBPAR PERFORMANCE · SEAL OF SUBPAR PERFORMANCE · SEAL OF SUB

Create your own humorous Air Travel Award by having a friend or a seatmate suggest words to fill in the blanks!

This award presented to _____
NAME OF RECIPIENT

on _____
TODAY'S DATE

for a trying day of Awful Air Travel

After paying extra for _____ at check-in,
PLURAL NOUN

_____ endured a full _____ patdown in the
NAME, AS ABOVE   PART OF THE BODY

security line. _____ then ate overpriced _____
NAME, AS ABOVE   PLURAL NOUN

in the concourse before boarding the flight, which was delayed

for _____ hours due to _____. Finally airborne,
NUMBER   WEATHER CONDITION

_____'s sanity was taxed by many passengers who
NAME, AS ABOVE

insisted on _____ loudly. Then there were all of the
VERB ENDING IN -ING

_____ children, and, of course, the always loathesome
ADJECTIVE

_____. When extreme _____
NAME OF A PERSON YOU KNOW   AN ACTIVITY

caused others to vomit, _____ did not
NAME, AS ABOVE

even _____. Even though everyone's
VERB

_____ went missing, _____
PLURAL NOUN   NAME, AS ABOVE

still managed a smile at the end of a very

stressful trip.

AWFUL AIR TRAVEL SURVIVOR AWARD

pg. 1

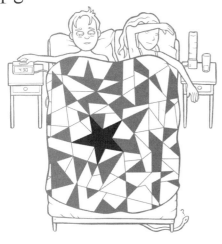

pg. 3

pg. 4

3	2	5	1	4	6
6	1	4	2	3	5
1	5	2	3	6	4
4	6	3	5	2	1
2	4	1	6	5	3
5	3	6	4	1	2

pg. 5

pg. 6-7

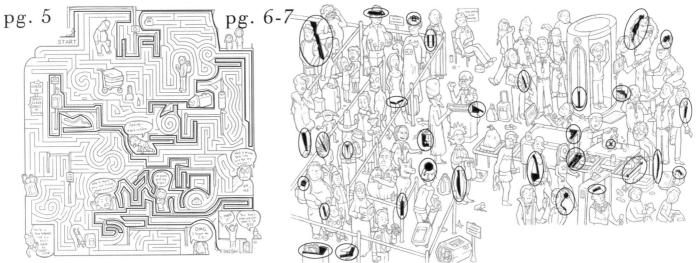

pg. 10

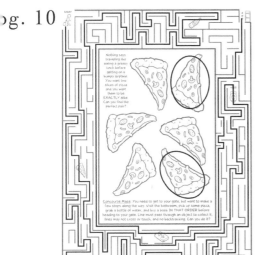

pg. 11

ALASKA
JETBLUE
SOUTHWEST
SPIRIT
UNITED
DELTA
ALLEGIANT
HAWAIIAN
AMERICAN
FRONTIER
VIRGIN

A BOEING
CONSTRICTOR

pg. 12

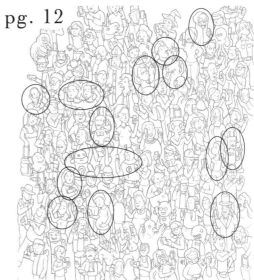

pg. 14

pg. 15

<u>Across:</u> 1. safety, 4. seated, 6. upright, 8. inflate, 10. smoke detector, 12. unlikely, 13. cabin, 15. caution

<u>Down:</u> 2. flight, 3. stow, 5. devices, 7. fastened, 9. arrival, 11. captain, 14. exit

EVEN MORE AWFUL SOLUTIONS

pg. 20

pg. 22

pg. 27

pg. 24

Security line,
Carry-on luggage,
Connecting flights,
Gate check,
Bumpy landing,
Initial descent,
Check-in counter,
Oversold flight,
First class,
Curbside check-in,
Traveling overseas,
Inflight magazine,
On-time arrival,
Overhead bin

pg. 26

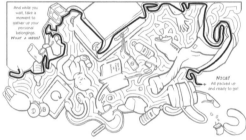

pg. 29

From left to right: Hungry, Anxious, Thirsty, Scared, Exhausted, Tired, Nauseous, Miserable